How to Check Out a Book

by Amanda StJohn

illustrated by Bob Ostrom

The Child's World®

Published by The Child's World®
1980 Lookout Drive • Mankato, MN 56003-1705
800-599-READ • www.childsworld.com

Acknowledgments
The Child's World®: Mary Berendes, Publishing Director
The Design Lab: Design and production
Red Line Editorial: Editorial direction

ISBN 9781614732495
LCCN 2012932864

Printed in the United States of America
Mankato, MN
July 2012
PA02127

About the Author

Amanda StJohn is an author and public librarian.
She's fascinated by singing frogs and animal tracks
and enjoys apricot tea and knitting.

About the Illustrator

Bob Ostrom is an award-winning children's
illustrator. His work has been featured in
more than two hundred children's books and
publications. When Bob is not illustrating children's
books you can usually find him in a classroom or
online teaching kids how to draw.

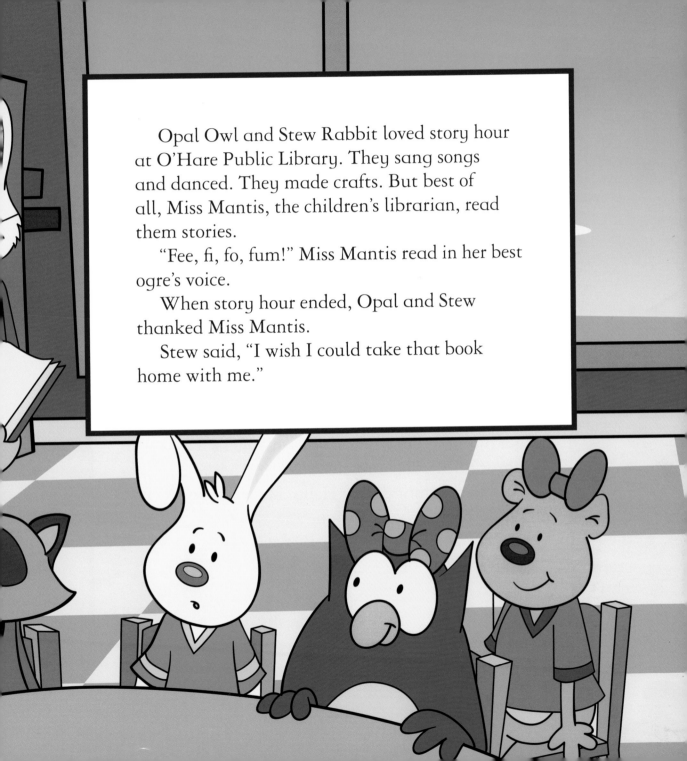

Opal Owl and Stew Rabbit loved story hour at O'Hare Public Library. They sang songs and danced. They made crafts. But best of all, Miss Mantis, the children's librarian, read them stories.

"Fee, fi, fo, fum!" Miss Mantis read in her best ogre's voice.

When story hour ended, Opal and Stew thanked Miss Mantis.

Stew said, "I wish I could take that book home with me."

"Jack and the Beanstalk?" asked Miss Mantis. "Of course you can borrow this book."

Stew's nose twitched. "You mean I can take it home?"

"She means you can check it out," Opal helped.

"Check it out?" Stew felt confused. He thought books had to stay in the library.

"Here," offered Opal, "I'll show you."

Miss Mantis handed Opal the book. From her mummy book bag, Opal pulled out a library card. She took her book and her library card to the front desk. "Hello, Mr. Badger," Opal greeted the librarian.

"Hi, Opal," smiled Mr. Badger. "May I have your library card?"

Opal gave Mr. Badger her library card. He **scanned** the card with a red laser beam. *Blip!* The computer bleeped.

Then Opal gave Mr. Badger her library book. He scanned the book with the red laser beam. *Blip!* The computer bleeped again.

"How was story hour?" Mr. Badger asked.

"It was a hoot!" whooped Opal.

Finally, a piece of paper popped up out of a small printer. "Here you go, Opal," chimed Mr. Badger. "Your book is due back in two weeks."

"Now we can take it home," Opal said to Stew.

"That's it?" Stew couldn't believe how easy it was to check out a book.

"Yeah!" Opal spread her wings. "Simple, right?"

Stew shook his head. "I don't understand. The computer went *blip, blip*—that's all. How did the computer know your name?"

"See this?" Opal showed Stew her library card. "It's my **bar code**. I'm the only one in the world with this bar code. Wave it under the scanner and—*blip!*—the computer knows my name."

"Okay," Stew prodded. "Then, how does the computer know which book you want?"

Opal laughed. "Every book in the library has its own bar code, too!"

"Really?" exclaimed Stew. "That's brilliant!"

"I know, right?" quipped Opal.

"Mr. Badger?" Stew asked. "May I have a library card?"

"Sure," said Mr. Badger. "Your father just has to agree."

Stew went and found his dad. "May I have a library card, pleeeeease?"

"You may," smiled Stew's dad. "Let's get you signed up."

At the front desk, Mr. Badger handed Stew's father a piece of paper.

"Will you fill out this **application**?" the librarian asked.

Stew and Opal were very excited. Stew hopped up and down—*boing, boing, boing.* Opal flapped her wings and a gust of wind blew papers off the desk.

"Uh, Mr. Badger," said Stew's father. "I think I will sit down and fill this out."

Sitting at a round table, Mr. Rabbit read the application aloud. "**Patron's** name."

"What's a patron?" asked Opal.

Mr. Rabbit answered, "A patron borrows library books. I'll write *Stew Rabbit*."

Mr. Rabbit read, "Patron's address." He wrote, "116 Carrot Patch Lane."

Stew read the next line. It said 'birthday.' "March 26," said Stew.

Opal read the last line on the paper. "My child can use this library card."

"I must sign there," explained Mr. Rabbit, and he wrote his name down.

Stew gave Mr. Badger the application. Mr. Badger gave Stew a library card. "Sign your name on it," he instructed.

Now that Stew had a card, he had to try it out. Stew found a funny book. He took the book and his library card to Mr. Badger. Mr. Badger scanned Stew's card with the red laser beam—*blip!* Then, he scanned the library book's bar code—*blip!* A little piece of paper popped out of a printer.

"Your book is due back in two weeks," noted Mr. Badger.

"Say," huffed Stew. "What is this piece of paper?"

Mr. Badger smiled. "It's called a **receipt**. It tells you when your books must be returned to the library."

"What if I don't return my book?"

"That's a great question," said Mr. Badger. "Does Opal know the answer?"

"Then, we'll have to pay a **fine** as a penalty," answered Opal.

"That's right," said Mr. Badger. "That's why you should keep your receipt and return your books on time."

"Got it," Stew nodded.

Just then, Opal and Stew heard a *blip, blip, blip!* But the sound wasn't coming from Mr. Badger's desk. Opal and Stew turned. The noise was coming from a row of computers with scanners.

Mr. Badger saw where they were looking and explained, "That's the self-checkout. You can check books out yourselves there."

"You mean I can do it all myself?" Opal's eyes were large as moons.

"Sure!" said Mr. Badger. "Go on and try."

Opal found a new book. This one was the story of two mice that lived beneath a woodpile. Opal and Stew went up to the self-checkout station.

"Now what?" Opal asked Stew.

"Zap your card with the laser beam!"

"Right!" Opal waved her library card under the scanner and the computer went *blip!* The computer read, "Hello, Opal Owl!"

"Woo-hooot!" she whooped.

"Is our book checked out?" asked Stew.

"No!" giggled Opal. "I just signed in. We have to scan the book."

"Let me try." Stew flipped the book around in his hands. He found the bar code—*blip!* "Wow!" he exclaimed.

"Hey," Opal whispered. "Stew, go get more books!"

In a short time, Stew returned with a large stack of books. *Blip, blip, blip!* Stew and Opal scanned books until the computer made an unhappy noise—*blomp!*

"Uh, oh!" gasped Opal.

"Did we break it?" worried Stew.

Mr. Badger poked his nose under the checkout desk and found Opal and Stew hiding there. "Hello," he said. "It's not broken. Come on out."

Mr. Badger didn't seem very angry. "Can you see the problem here?"

Stew and Opal saw a note on the computer screen. Stew sounded out the words, "Over your limit."

"Over your limit?" repeated Opal.

"Yes," said Mr. Badger. "Each patron is allowed ten books at one time."

"So we picked too many books?" asked Stew.

Mr. Badger agreed. "And don't forget, these books go home with Opal."

"Oh." Opal understood. "Because we used my card."

Mr. Badger smiled, "You got it!"

Opal and Stew did not leave a mess. They set the extra books on a book cart. They said bye to Mr. Badger and Miss Mantis. Then, they strapped on bicycle helmets and tucked away their books.

"What will we do next?" Opal asked Stew.

"We'll make our own story hour," beamed Stew. "We'll invite our moms!"

Glossary

application (ap-li-KAY-shun): An application is the sign-up form for a library card. Stew's dad filled out Stew's library card application.

bar code (BAR KODE): A bar code is a series of vertical lines that identify a patron, book, or media. There is a bar code on Opal's library card.

fine (FINE): A fine is money you pay if you damage, lose, or return a library book late. Stew will have to pay a fine if he doesn't return his library books on time.

patron (PAY-trun): A patron is a person who uses the library. Stew and Opal are library patrons.

receipt (ri-SEET): A receipt is a small slip of paper that tells you when to return your books. Mr. Badger gave Stew a receipt when he checked out books.

scan (SKAN): To scan is to wave a bar code under a laser. Mr. Badger scans books to check them out.

Tips to Remember!

- Treat your book nicely.

- Hug your book to your chest to carry it without dropping it.

- Always wash your hands before handling books.

- Books don't like to get wet! Keep them away from sinks, bathtubs, and rain.

- Don't color or write in books.

- Use bookmarks.

Web Sites

Visit our Web site for links about library skills: childsworld.com/links

Note to Parents, Teachers, and Librarians: We routinely verify our Web links to make sure they are safe and active sites. So encourage your readers to check them out!

Books

Blue, Rose. *Ron's Big Mission*. New York: Dutton Children's, 2009.

Hubbell, Patricia. *Check It Out!: Reading, Finding, Helping*. Tarrytown, NY: Marshall Cavendish, 2011.

Steward, Sarah. *The Library*. New York: Square Fish, 2008.